THE APPRENTICE WITCH

Text by
Robyn Valentine

Illustrations by
Flavia Sorrentino

DOVER PUBLICATIONS
Garden City, New York

CONTENTS

SPELLS

P. 60

JOURNAL

P. 87

BEFORE
READING

What does it mean to be a witch? Well, there are lots of different answers, depending on whom you are speaking with. Witchcraft can take on a variety of paths and traditions. For this reason, different people assign different meanings to the title of the witch.

In short, a witch is someone who uses their inner energy and the energy all around them to make a change, through spellwork or rituals. A witch is an individual who puts their intention out into the universe to get the outcomes that they would like in their life.

A witch may be somebody who has a dedicated daily routine, one where they offer up their energy. Or they may be somebody who creates potions in their cauldron to ace a test. Witches use herbs, nature, the universe, incantations, and other tools to see the outcomes they want in the world and peer into the future.

Regardless of how you personally define the word, witches are empowered people who know that their strength comes from within. We are all unique, and this uniqueness can bring forth the things we want to see in the world—whether that's protecting your home, mending a friendship, or finding purpose in your daily routine. Perhaps you want to learn to read fortunes or create healing spells for your family. Anyone can be a witch, as long as they're willing to put time and energy into their spellwork and know that all things can happen as long as we believe in ourselves.

CONNECTING WITH NATURE

As a witch, one of the simplest ways to connect with magic is to learn to tap into the power of nature, no matter where you live!

While not every witch will have a garden or even a community park that they can visit easily, every witch has the ability to bring a little nature into their life! Although not every witch works with natural frequencies, it is every witch's duty to tend to Mother Earth in one way or another.

How this is done will look different for every witch. REMEMBER: NO MATTER HOW LARGE OR SMALL YOUR CONTRIBUTIONS ARE, EVERY LITTLE BIT COUNTS.

LET'S START!

✴GROWING YOUR OWN WINDOWSILL GARDEN

Seeds from leftover meals or even a dried bean can be grown right on your windowsill, to bring a little plant life right to you. Sometimes the simple act of caring for windowsill foliage will help you feel **MORE CONNECTED TO THE ENERGIES OF NATURE.**

✴NEIGHBORHOOD CLEANUP

Whether you live in a bustling city or a rural village, litter seems to follow us everywhere. Take a walk with your parent or guardian, and bring a trash bag with you. Make it a goal to fill the whole thing on your walk! Even if you don't come back with a full bag, you're doing an amazing thing for nature in your community.

✴LEARN ABOUT THE LOCAL FLORA

The plants in your neighborhood are bursting with energy, and learning about their magical and practical properties is fascinating. You may find that people from thousands of years ago used the same plants for something special! You might not find all the local flora, but it'll still be fun to try to spot them when you're out and about.

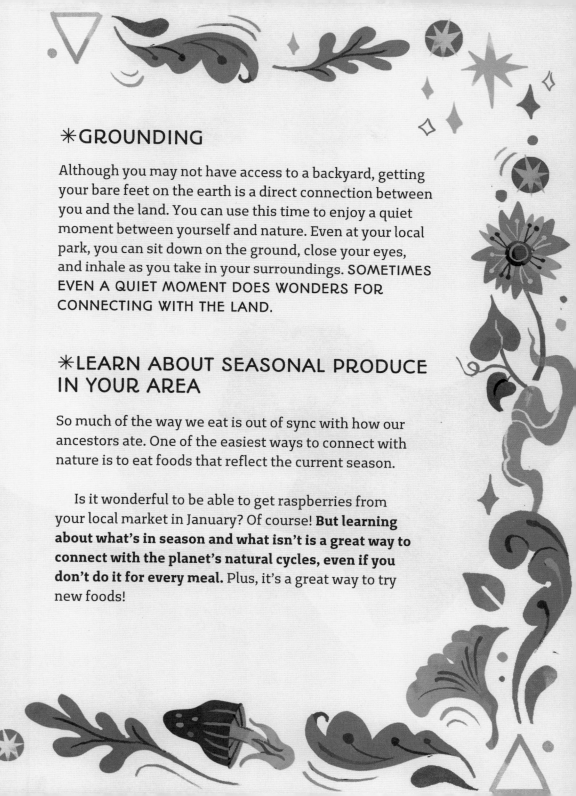

✳GROUNDING

Although you may not have access to a backyard, getting your bare feet on the earth is a direct connection between you and the land. You can use this time to enjoy a quiet moment between yourself and nature. Even at your local park, you can sit down on the ground, close your eyes, and inhale as you take in your surroundings. SOMETIMES EVEN A QUIET MOMENT DOES WONDERS FOR CONNECTING WITH THE LAND.

✳LEARN ABOUT SEASONAL PRODUCE IN YOUR AREA

So much of the way we eat is out of sync with how our ancestors ate. One of the easiest ways to connect with nature is to eat foods that reflect the current season.

Is it wonderful to be able to get raspberries from your local market in January? Of course! **But learning about what's in season and what isn't is a great way to connect with the planet's natural cycles, even if you don't do it for every meal.** Plus, it's a great way to try new foods!

MAKING YOUR OWN PATH

Because each witch defines their craft in their own words, there are a few things to consider when you get started. First and foremost, witchcraft has a variety of traditions that might shape the kind of witch you become. We are going to touch upon a couple of styles that might be of interest to you, but you don't have to put a label on your practice. You can simply be a witch! But for some people, starting off with a specific label or category is important. And that's more than okay too! So, if you were to label yourself, what kind of witch would you be? While they aren't the only paths available to witches, here are a few that might interest you.

WHAT KIND OF WITCH ARE YOU?

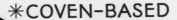

✳COVEN-BASED

Covens are often found in Wicca, a modern, earth-based Pagan religion, but many groups use joint efforts to conjure magic.

FORMING A COVEN WITH FRIENDS IS A GREAT WAY TO TAP INTO STRENGTH IN NUMBERS, AND LEARNING TOGETHER CAN OFTEN YIELD CREATIVE RESULTS.

Many established coven spaces are designed for adults. If this is something you're interested in, talk to your parent or guardian before entering any spaces involving strangers.

✳GREEN

Green witches rely on their plant companions to help them with their magic.

GREEN WITCHES MIGHT HAVE GARDENS, WORK A LOT WITH LOCAL HERBS, OR JUST HAVE A DEEP-ROOTED INTEREST IN HERBALISM.

*HEDGE WITCH

A hedge witch works between the space of the spirit world and our world. In the past, a "hedge" marked the physical boundary of a village or town, and thus symbolically divided our physical reality and the spirit world.

HEDGE WITCHES USUALLY WORK ALONE—THEY'RE "SOLITARIES"—AND HAVE LEARNED BY DOING OR FROM ONE-ON-ONE SESSIONS WITH SOMEONE MORE EXPERIENCED.

They rely heavily on nature and their intuition.

*ECLECTIC

Eclectic witches are those who pick up things that work for them, from a variety of traditions.

MANY ECLECTIC WITCHES WORK WITH NATURE, NOT GODS, DEITIES, OR SPIRITS.

They may ask the universe for guidance in the craft, and they don't feel the need to stick to one tradition.

*KITCHEN WITCH

A kitchen witch enjoys making their home and surroundings a sacred space.

THEY LIKE TO INCORPORATE WITCHCRAFT INTO THEIR COOKING AND CHANNEL THEIR ENERGY INTO THE FOOD AND THE MEALS THEY CREATE.

Creating your own herb garden for kitchen spells is a great way to put intention into your cooking, from start to finish.

*FOLK WITCH

Folk witches are centered around FOLKLORE AND TRADITIONS, BASED ON THE RELIGIONS, LEGENDS, MYSTICISM, AND LORE of a region or culture from anywhere in the world.

* SEA WITCH

Sea witches rely on the sea and its natural resources, as well as on the energy of the Moon, which also influences the tides.

THE SEA SWELLS AND SHRINKS EVERY DAY, MUCH LIKE THE MOON'S PHASES.

Sea witches harness this energy to perform their spells.

* ELEMENTAL WITCH

Elemental witches include the energy and magic of the four **ELEMENTS** as the basis of their practice: **FIRE, WATER, EARTH,** and **AIR.**

They call to these elements and their aligned intentions in their spellwork, and they find symbolism in each element to represent their goals.

STILL DON'T KNOW WHAT KIND OF PATH MIGHT INTEREST YOU?

HERE ARE SOME FACTORS THAT MAY BE WORTH EXPLORING!

*WHERE ARE YOUR ANCESTORS FROM?

You may not know! You also may not care. And both are totally okay! But if you're interested in folk magic, learning about legends and folklore from your ancestors' homeland might be a great place to start. If you can, talk to an older relative, like a grandparent. Where are they from? Are there any local legends from that area? Check it out! It's important to note that a lot of people do not have a connection to their ancestors, so this isn't a necessary path, just something that can potentially be explored.

✳HAVE YOU HEARD OF SPIRITS IN EVERYTHING?

Some paths hold that there is energy or a spirit in everything found in nature. This is called animism. Exploring the spirits outside is a great way to work with energy that's around you at all times.

NO MATTER WHERE YOU GO, EVEN IN THE BUSIEST OF CITIES, YOU CAN SEEK OUT THE SPIRIT OF THAT PLACE.

✳WORKING WITH THE UNIVERSE, OR THE "DIVINE" IN GENERAL, IS ALWAYS A SOLID OPTION

Some people prefer to work with the great beyond. It has no name or face; there is no god or deity. Instead, they turn to "the universe," meaning everything we cannot see, what we can only understand spiritually. Across cultures and life paths, opinions on the universe vary. Because it is all-encompassing, and has no agenda or moral code, the universe is great for someone who isn't sure what kind of path they want to follow.

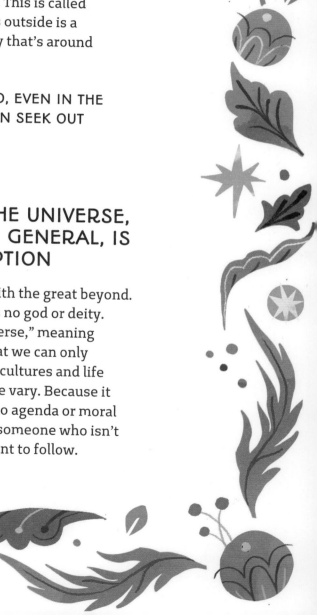

MAKING AN ALTAR

A witch's altar is the most sacred of spaces. It's where the "spirit sits," the place around which you create your own MAGICAL BARRIER from the outside world, a place where you might cast your SPELLS, write in your witch's journal, read TAROT cards, and so much more. If you want to work with different types of guides, such as deities, ancestors, saints, or spirits, you might dedicate this space to them. If an activity is magical and requires your energy, this is the place to do it.

Altar spaces can be on a bookshelf, your windowsill, or even a simple shoebox. It depends on what works for you! While you may see older, more experienced witches with elaborate, grand altars, don't worry! That's something they've created over time. INSTEAD, WE'LL START SMALL, PRACTICALLY, AND EVEN TUCKED AWAY.

The items on your altar should represent the energies you're working with. Altars can also be set up temporarily, for an intention. So, while your sacred space may be put away between uses, it's still there when you need it.

✳EARTH

Earth is everywhere. It seems passive, as it doesn't really "do" anything, at least not with the same force as Air, Fire, or Water. Yet, we are born of Earth. While we are alive, it sustains us. When we die, it covers us. Earth encompasses a multitude of magical ideas: nourishment, protection, obstruction, wholeness, stillness, plant and animal life, interdependence, prosperity, and rest.

✳WATER

Water is the great partner of Earth in creating life as we know it. Like Earth, Water seems gentle, but it contains immense potential power. It is cleansing, calming, and healing. Water also controls the magic of love and emotion, intuition, and introspection. Water is directly connected to the Moon.

Pentacles; the altar (base) itself; ceramics; cast metal; coins; rocks and crystals; dishes of soil, sand, or salt; cauldrons; horn or bone; acorns, seeds, Images of trees and mountains; gnomes; animal art (cattle, tortoises, rabbits, deer)

Chalices; cups; beverages (especially water); crystal balls; rainwater; seashells; driftwood or seaweed; a mirror; mermaids; images of the ocean, rivers, or lakes; animal art (fish, dolphins, frogs)

Traditionally, witches keep symbols of the four elements on their altar. A few altar ideas are found below, but your altar can be as changeable and unique as you are!

*FIRE

As an element, Fire is the pure power of heat and light. The energy of Fire is strong, primal, and dangerous. In Fire, we find the heat of passion and the warrior's fighting spirit. Fire's energy includes courage, willpower, protection, spiritual aspiration, destruction, and impending renewal. Fire is associated with the Sun and its life-giving power.

Wands; flames (candles and oil lamps); incense (doubles for both Air and Fire); cacti or thorns; dragons; images of flames or the Sun; volcanic stones or ashes; bright yellow or orange plants; animal art (lions, lizards, a phoenix)

*AIR

As Air passes over the still Earth, the world moves into action and consciousness. Air is the element of communication, exchange, and ideas. Air is invisible: we know it exists only through its effects on the world. Air is also swift-moving, changeable, and self-aware. It is the most human of all the Elements.

Athames (witches' daggers), wands, or staffs; feathers; wind chimes; bells; incense; lamps or lanterns (knowledge); fans; books; spoons; wheels; brightly colored ribbon or streamers; images of clouds or the sky; animal art (birds, dragonflies, butterflies); angels; fairies; air fresheners or diffusers

A WITCH'S APOTHECARY IN THE KITCHEN

Early on in your journey through witchcraft, you may be wondering what kind of HERBS you need. Throughout history, magic practitioners often had TO HIDE IN PLAIN SIGHT, which means they used what they had available to them. That could have been anything from backyard weeds to spices and herbs found in the KITCHEN PANTRY.

A little goes a long way, so please don't clear out your family's pantry to cast a spell. A pinch of this and a dash of that is all you need to get big results! While the following pages are not a complete list of all the herbs and spices you could use, they do contain some COMMON WITCHCRAFT INGREDIENTS that you probably have access to without even realizing it.

COMMON WITCHCRAFT INGREDIENTS

✳ SALT

This is the simplest protection ingredient in any pantry. Sprinkle some in the corners of your room to keep negative energy away. Or mix Moon Water (see page 75) and a pinch of salt, then spray it on yourself (lightly) to form a shield against unwanted vibrations. Use it to wash away negative energy by adding it to your bath!

✳ PEPPER

Pepper is a great protective herb. It can be added to spell jars to protect your room from unwanted energies or kept in your pocket to ensure you are safe.

✳ ROSEMARY

Rosemary is an all-purpose herb. Traditionally used for protection and cleansing, rosemary can be a substitute for an herb you might be missing in recipes.

✳ BASIL

Basil is traditionally used for money-related magic, but it can be used for all sorts of abundance. Perhaps you're hoping to raise money at school or you're trying to win a prize. Mix a bit of basil with other lucky herbs and there you have it: the basis for a powerful spell. Basil can also be used to lift a mood. If you and a friend are fighting and you want to break the ice and heal your friendship, basil can give you the courage you need.

✳ BAY LEAVES

Bay leaves can be burned to make your wishes come true. **But please don't burn anything without supervision, as it can be very unsafe!** Bay is all about manifesting and seeing your wishes come true. Write your wish on a bay leaf and add it to your spell jars, or burn it in a safe space over a cauldron or fireproof bowl. You can keep the ashes and use them for future spells that call for the same energy.

✳ THYME

Thyme is terrific for magic related to healing. Maybe you're feeling under the weather or a family member has a cold. Using thyme as a key ingredient in magic aimed at a speedy recovery is ideal.

✳ORANGE PEEL

Orange peel is great for clarity and protection. Have some tea with orange peels in it before practicing divination (foreseeing future events). If you slice orange peels thin and dry them in the oven (ask an adult for help!), they can be hung in the windows to keep negativity away. Add orange peels to candles or spell jars kept near your sacred space.

✳CINNAMON

Cinnamon is used for magic related to money and protection. Keep a stick of cinnamon in your piggy bank to find unexpected money. Hang a stick of cinnamon above your door to keep unwanted energy out. Sweep your room with cinnamon to push away unwanted energy.

✳DILL

If you have nightmares or are scared of ghosts, dill is terrific! It helps keep nightmares and bad entities away. This herb will ward off unwanted spirits and keep bad dreams at bay.

✳FENNEL

If you are going to a faraway place and are nervous about traveling, fennel can ensure a safe return. Fennel is excellent for safe travel, especially for friends and family. Use it in spellwork that involves a safe journey for you or a loved one.

✳LAVENDER

Lavender can be used for friendships and to create a calm space. If you want to have good dreams, keeping a sachet of lavender under your pillow can help you sleep better and bring you sweet dreams. If communication is a problem in a friendship, keep some lavender in your pocket when you hang out with that person. It will help communication flow better and keep conversations positive.

✳ALLSPICE

Allspice is great in a pinch when you need a little luck. If you didn't study as hard as you could have, or if you've entered a contest, allspice is the perfect ingredient for spellwork when you want to conjure good fortune.

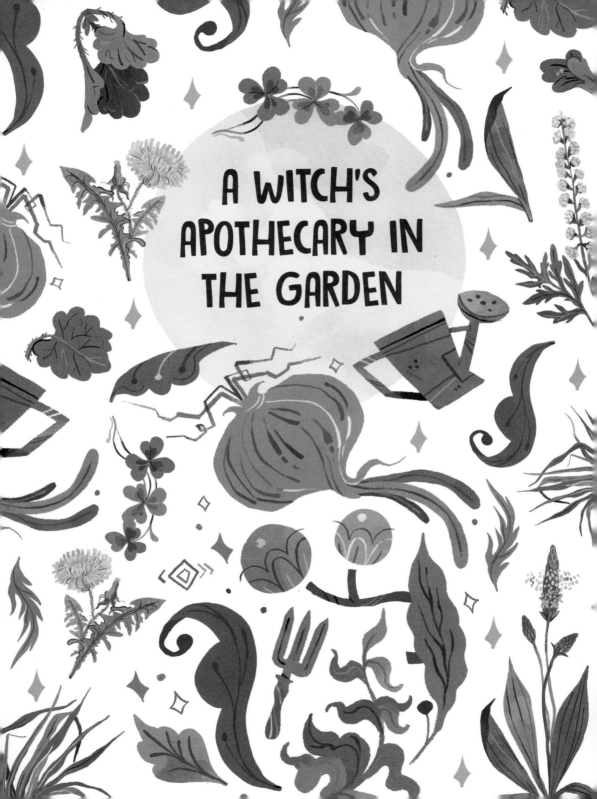

A WITCH'S APOTHECARY IN THE GARDEN

Before you raid your pantry, head out to your garden. There might be powerful herbs already growing there! Common backyard weeds found all over the world have a lot of magical properties. Remember: a weed is just a plant growing where it isn't wanted. AS WITCHES, WE MIGHT FIND THAT WEEDS BECOME SACRED MAGICAL PLANTS, GIVEN NEW PURPOSES.

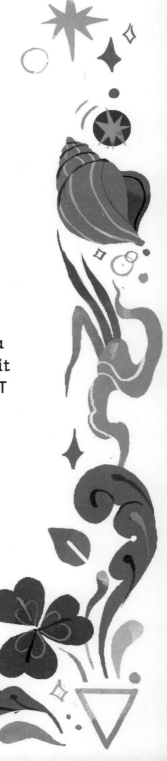

POWERFUL HERBS

✳CLOVER

Clover is found in many forms: white clover, red clover, four-leaf clover, etc. Each one has slightly different properties. Generally speaking, clover is used for good luck spells, protection, money, love, and success.

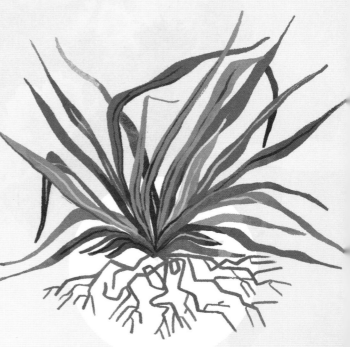

✳CRABGRASS

Crabgrass is a pesky lawn "weed" with deep roots that make it nearly impossible to get rid of. For this reason, it's great when used in spells that require stability, determination, durability, and overall power.

✳DANDELION

You may have blown on a dandelion to make a wish. This plant has a long history of powerful magic. Dandelions can be used as a psychic aid, or brewed into a tea that's consumed before divination sessions, like tarot cards and crystal ball readings, known as scrying.

✳PLANTAIN WEED

Greater plantain leaves have a long history of healing properties, as they sometimes are edible. **Please don't eat them, though. You don't know what pesticides may have been sprayed on them.** Plantain leaves are used in spells for healing, strength, protection, and mending friendships.

✳ RAGWEED

Ragweed's magical properties are minimal. This plant is used medicinally for healing a wide range of wounds. It's also good for quick recovery spells, as well as courage.

✳ GOLDENROD

Although many people are allergic to goldenrod, it can be a source of good fortune. Its properties include luck, money, and prosperity.

*GROUND IVY

This beautiful but invasive plant is closely connected to the Moon. Its magical properties are not vast, but they are powerful. Ground ivy is ideal for divination, intuition, and protection from overwhelming situations.

*MULLEIN

This invasive plant is found across the globe, brought to different countries by colonists. It is also known as a hag's torch because this tall plant was once used in magic, dipping the stalks in tallow to then light them as candles. Mullein is a great herb for protection, health, and cleansing.

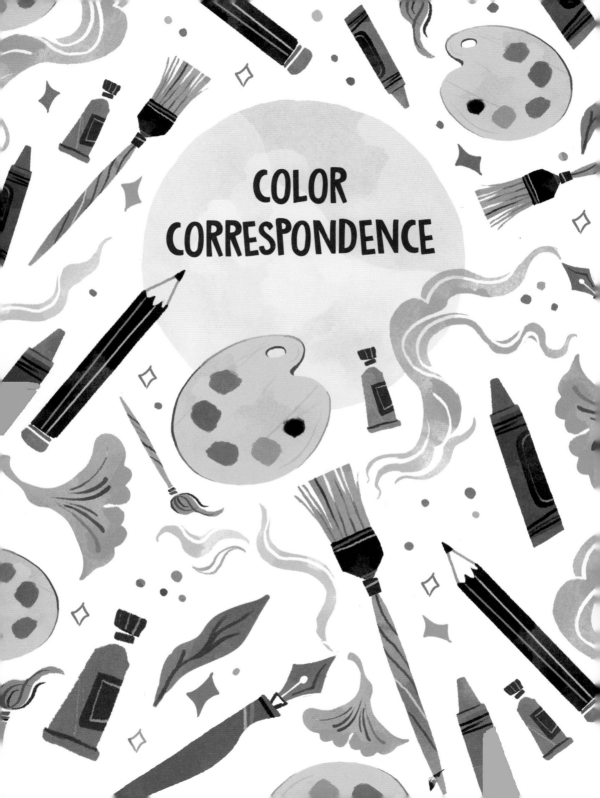

COLOR CORRESPONDENCE

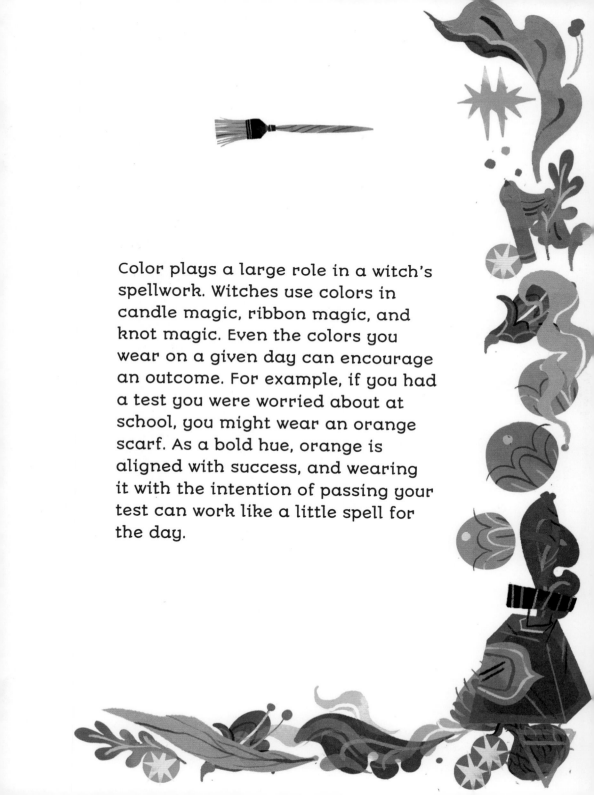

Color plays a large role in a witch's spellwork. Witches use colors in candle magic, ribbon magic, and knot magic. Even the colors you wear on a given day can encourage an outcome. For example, if you had a test you were worried about at school, you might wear an orange scarf. As a bold hue, orange is aligned with success, and wearing it with the intention of passing your test can work like a little spell for the day.

✳WHITE

Purity, truth, sincerity, protection, cleansing, Full Moon rituals, meditation, peace, sincerity, justice, warding off doubts and fears.

✳PURPLE

Tension, ambition, power, progress, power, spiritual development, intuition, healing, spiritual communication, protection.

✳SILVER

Lunar magic, meditation, psychic abilities, success, balance, warding off negativity.

✳BLUE

Tranquility, understanding, patience, health, impulsiveness, change, intuition, opportunity, understanding, safe journeys, Water element.

✳BLACK

Cleansing, warding off negativity, removing hexes, protection, spirit contact, night, truth, removing discord or confusion, clearing the mind, meditation.

✳GREEN

Finance, luck, friendship, Earth element, healing, balance, work and employment, courage, agriculture, changing direction or attitudes.

*RED

Strength, health, Fire element, power, energy, enthusiasm, courage.

*PINK

Honor, morality, friendship, emotional love.

*ORANGE

Encouragement, attraction, success, strength, healing, adaptability, luck, vitality, encouragement, clearing the mind.

*BROWN

Hesitation, uncertainty, neutrality, endurance, animal health, steadiness, houses and homes, physical objects, uncertainties.

*YELLOW

Attraction, charm, persuasion, confidence, Air element, divination, clairvoyance, mental alertness, intellectual growth, prosperity, learning, changes, harmony, creativity, concentration.

*GOLD

Solar energy, power, physical strength, success, achievement, mental growth, a skill sought, healing energy, intuition, divination, fortune, warding off negativity.

*GRAY

Erasure, neutrality, stalemate.

CRYSTALS

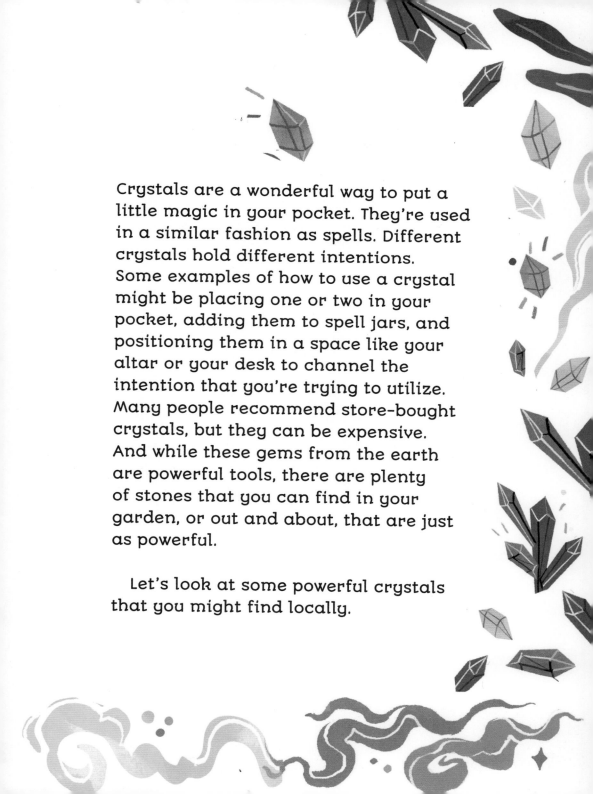

Crystals are a wonderful way to put a little magic in your pocket. They're used in a similar fashion as spells. Different crystals hold different intentions. Some examples of how to use a crystal might be placing one or two in your pocket, adding them to spell jars, and positioning them in a space like your altar or your desk to channel the intention that you're trying to utilize. Many people recommend store-bought crystals, but they can be expensive. And while these gems from the earth are powerful tools, there are plenty of stones that you can find in your garden, or out and about, that are just as powerful.

Let's look at some powerful crystals that you might find locally.

HOW TO USE DIFFERENT CRYSTALS

✳ QUARTZ

A wide variety of quartz can be found all over the world, from clear quartz and amethyst to rare specimens. In most places around the globe, you'll find at least one kind of quartz in your yard, possibly even in your flower beds! For our purposes, the quartz you find near your home can be used as a spell booster. It will enhance spells and make your magic even more powerful.

✳ RIVER ROCK

If you head to a river or a local lake, you might happen upon lots of smooth stones. Because of where they are found, river rocks can be an easy way to channel energy, practice grounding, bring about peace, and redirect your emotions.

✳ SEA GLASS

Found on many beaches, sea glass is man-made glass that has been tumbled by the ocean waves, creating a sort of smooth stone. Sea glass is a symbol of renewal and healing. You might use this sea glass when you are starting a new project, and need a little confidence to see it through.

✳GRANITE

Different types of granite are found all over the world. In some places, granite chips are used as landscaping elements. While you might not find granite naturally, you might still have some nearby. Granite is used for magical situations where you need to create more balance in a relationship or cooperation in a group setting. If you are working on a school project with a group of friends, for example, keeping a bit of granite in your pocket would ensure smooth communication and a balanced workload.

✳OBSIDIAN

Obsidian is a perfect stone for protecting one's energy. This black, glassy stone is found in places that are close to volcanoes. It's used to protect your energy from outside influences, and to keep you safe in any situation that might give you anxiety.

✳PUMICE/LAVA ROCK

Lightweight yet rough to touch, this stone is very good at absorbing negative energy. Much like the stone's ability to absorb water and scrub off rough, unwanted skin, pumice works well in purifying situations. You might keep a bit of pumice stone in your school desk or backpack as a sponge for negative energy from bullies. If you're nervous about a test, keep some nearby to absorb your own negative vibes that are keeping you on edge.

LUNAR PHASES

The Moon is connected to intuition as well as magical mysteries. It's a celestial body that has a long-standing history of being used in magic to further intentions for spellwork. Although not all spells have to be aligned with the lunar phases, when they are, that alignment can help you see an intention fulfilled. WITCHES WORK WITH SIX PHASES OF THE MOON: NEW, WAXING, FULL, WANING, CRYING, AND DARK MOON. CRYING and DARK MOONS are used in very powerful and often negative magic. It's the only way to utilize those lunar phases, so, for our purposes, we won't cover them here. A full cycle of the lunar month takes about 29 days. Early civilizations often based their calendars around the cycles of the Moon, rather than modern calendars, which are based on the revolution of the Earth around the Sun.

PHASES OF THE MOON

✳FULL MOON

This is the phase of the Moon that most people are comfortable working with. The Full Moon is the part of the lunar cycle when energy is at its peak. It is therefore utilized in this intense form most frequently. Each Full Moon spans a three-day period.

SO, IF YOU'RE AFRAID YOU MISSED IT, REMEMBER THAT THE DAY BEFORE AND THE DAY AFTER THE MOON IS AT 100% ALSO COUNT AS FULL MOON DAYS.

✳WANING MOON

Waning refers to when the Moon's visibility is shrinking. A Waning Moon begins after the third Full Moon day and lasts all the way until the night before New Moon.

BECAUSE OF THE NATURE OF A WANING MOON SHRINKING IN VISIBILITY, USE THIS TIME TO PUSH AWAY OR "SHRINK" ENERGIES IN YOUR LIFE THAT YOU DON'T WANT.

✳WAXING MOON

The Waxing Moon occurs the day after the New Moon and lasts all the way until the day before the Full Moon. During this phase, the Moon gives off the illusion of being bigger and brighter than it normally is, and the Moon looks like it's growing night after night.

AS THE MOON GROWS, IT ATTRACTS. THEREFORE THE WAXING MOON IS AN APPROPRIATE TIME FOR MAGIC THAT ATTRACTS.

✳NEW MOON

The New Moon is the first sliver that appears after the Moon is completely black, also known as the Dark Moon. This is a time for beginnings, launching new projects, and fresh starts. The New Moon only lasts one night, and therefore it is often missed.

IF YOU CATCH THE NEW MOON, IT'S A GREAT TIME TO PRACTICE MAGIC THAT IS CENTERED AROUND NEW PROJECTS, GOALS, AND LONG-TERM GROWTH.

MAGIC DAYS

Every day of the week is a magical day. Much like the Moon's phases, you can utilize what day you cast a spell to further your intention. Especially if you are caught in a time where you can't track the changing Moon, tapping into the days of the week is a great substitute. PAIRING A LUNAR PHASE WITH THE DAY OF THE WEEK WILL MAKE YOUR SPELL EVEN MORE POTENT THAN JUST ONE COMPONENT ALONE.

DAYS OF THE WEEK

MONDAY

This day of the week is dedicated to the Moon and all of her magic and mystery. Mondays are for mysteries, illusions, prophecies, emotions, and travel.

TUESDAY

Tuesday is a day dedicated to courage, rebellion, and strength. If you are facing a challenge of any kind, need a boost to your courage, or want to enhance what you're passionate about, align your magic with Tuesday.

WEDNESDAY

Wednesdays are for communication, change, cunning, and the arts. This is a day full of contradictions, change, and excitement. Align your spellwork with Wednesday for excitement, and whenever you seek dramatic changes in your favor.

THURSDAY

When you are looking for the day of the week that's ideal for prosperity, abundance, luck, and good health, look no further than Thursday. As this day is also named after the Norse god Thor, Thursdays are great for strength.

FRIDAY

Friday is a day that is dedicated to many love and fertility goddesses around the world. This day of the week is for magical topics such as love, birth (including art projects and ideas), and romance.

SATURDAY

This day is associated with protection and banishing a negative situation, and it is a good time to clean up any magical messes that you have been ignoring. If someone was bullying you at school and you'd like it to stop, consider spellwork on a Saturday.

SUNDAY

Sunday corresponds to the Sun. This day is potent for spellwork in success, wealth, and fame. Sundays are for personal achievements and seeing goals through to their finish. If you want to attract the attention of someone, consider spellwork on this day. Just like the Sun's rays, any projects you are trying to see grow can be magically nourished at this time.

GROUNDING

What is grounding?

The term is used in both witchcraft and mental health terminology. Grounding is a practice that witches and nonpractitioners use to cleanse themselves spiritually or to connect with the earth, washing away excess energy. In times of stress or anxiety, grounding is a way to release unwanted energy from yourself. It is a great way to rid yourself of excess energy or reroot your energy after spellwork. UTILIZE THE EARTH AS A MEANS OF DOING SO.

GROUNDING TECHNIQUES

✳ROOTING VISUALIZATION

This is probably the most commonly used grounding technique, and it is the simplest.
ALL YOU NEED IS A QUIET MOMENT AND YOUR MIND. To ground yourself and release unwanted energy, sit in a comfortable position, with your bones connecting to the ground below you. Flatten the palms of your hands on the ground or floor. Alternatively, you can lie down, placing your body flat on the ground. I recommend trying to press your spine flat along the earth if you can, ignoring its natural curve. Take three deep breaths.

Visualize the energy flowing from the top of your head; through your body, specifically your hands and backside; and into the earth. You can do the visualization in reverse, pulling energy from the ground and upward into your body. I like to visualize the energy turning into roots that extend into the earth, firmly planting myself there.

Another way to do this is TO STAND UP. In this version, point your hands downward, standing stiff and straight. In yoga, this position would look like Mountain Pose. Visualize roots reaching out from your fingertips and the soles of your feet, planting themselves in the ground. Again, if done in reverse, the roots become branches, and they grow from the ground, wrapping around your feet and hands.

✳APPLE CIDER VINEGAR

THIS TECHNIQUE WILL REQUIRE SOME ADVANCE PLANNING. This is a technique I like to do once a month—plus, it's good for your hair and skin. **YOU WILL NEED APPLE CIDER VINEGAR (ACV) AND ACCESS TO A BATH OR SHOWER.** After combining 6 parts water and 1 part ACV, pour this mixture over your head. I recommend either using hot water or leaving the ACV on a shelf for a while beforehand, so that it's at room temperature. I prefer to do this in the shower, standing, while the water isn't hitting me at that moment, which is why it's important to warm up the water first, at least a little. If not, the cold mixture may be a bit of a shock! The acidity of the ACV helps to get rid of excess energy, but it also removes lingering impurities from the skin—metaphysically, not literally. I pour it on my head and quietly meditate for a moment before rinsing it off.

✳HEALING BATH

Draw up a warm bath and add some Epsom salt, not only for muscle relaxation but also for cleansing and purity. Add some baking soda for the same effect. Keep the ratio of 3 parts salt and 1 part baking soda. You can also use Florida water instead of baking soda. You can even add herbs that align with cleansing and protecting properties. Suggestions include lemon rinds, rosemary, lavender, sage, and mugwort.

Stay in the bath as long as you'd like, but take some quiet moments to visualize excess energy leaving your body. A great way to do this is to visualize a white light washing over you. I recommend using a reusable tea bag for any loose herbs or using a strainer to scoop them up before you drain your bath.

*SHOWER

This is something I highly recommend, as it's easy to do: a cedar shower. Take a branch of clean *Y*-shaped cedar; soak your branch in a bath overnight, killing any bugs that may be in it. Then hang the branch over your showerhead. This may be something that you've seen with eucalyptus. When you take a shower, hold it over your back, letting the water hit the branch and then run down your body. Hang the cedar branch back up in between uses, and as a bonus, your shower and bathroom will smell like you just stepped into a forest on a rainy day.

SPELLS

WRITING YOUR OWN SPELLS

No two witches will tell you the same instructions for how to write spells. It's something that you develop as an individual over time. For some, speaking an incantation creates a powerful spell. For others, focusing their intention on candle-based spells may be better. The beauty of witchcraft is that no two practitioners follow the exact same rules. Many witches, at least when they first start out, are afraid to come up with their own spells, for fear of something going wrong. Luckily, while you are figuring out spellwork, it's unlikely you will do anything so powerful that it can't be undone. Being brave enough to write your own spells will always get more powerful and successful outcomes than merely following someone else's. EVEN ADDING YOUR OWN SPECIAL TOUCHES TO OTHERS' SPELLS WILL MAKE THEM UNIQUELY YOUR OWN.

STEP-BY-STEP

✳PLAN

First, map out how the spell will be done. Make a list and note whether the ingredients, colors, materials, etc., match the purpose and intention of your spell. THIS IS THE MOST CRUCIAL PART OF ANY SPELL, RITUAL, OR CHARM.

Although it's true that everyone will have elements that correspond to different degrees, do your best to align your ingredients with your intentions. Depending on the kind of magic you are performing, your ingredients will vary. Start by understanding the basics of how they correspond, and let it grow from there. Shortcuts from the beginning will only lead to frustration and disappointment.

✳INSCRIBE

ARE YOU DOING A CANDLE SPELL? Inscribe the objects used in your spell, as needed, that align with your goals or the energies you are working with. This can be anything from a rune, elemental symbols, written names, etc.

*PERFORM

It's important early on to pay attention to *when* you perform your spell. Align your intentions with lunar phases and days of the week, to make sure your spellwork has the highest possible success rate.

*VISUALIZE

Knowing the spell will work before you have even begun is key to being successful. You are a strong, powerful witch. Why wouldn't it work?

VISUALIZING THE SPELL AS COMPLETED AND SUCCESSFUL, BEFORE YOU BEGIN, IS THE FIRST STEP TO SUCCESS.

*DISPOSE

Last but not least, how you dispose of your spellwork tools can be just as crucial as the spell itself. You may need to carry around your charm, or burn it and throw the ashes into a crossroads. Consider if the spell can be buried or thrown in the trash. If you are going to bury your spell, make sure your vessels and ingredients won't hurt the environment: witches never, ever litter!

PERSONAL PROTECTION

THIS SPELL PROTECTS YOU FROM EMOTIONAL HARM.

Day: Saturday
Time: Night or Waxing/Full Moon

You will need the following:
- Salt ▪ A picture or drawing of yourself
- Plantain or dill ▪ Dish
- Bowl and spoon, or mortar and pestle

Start by mixing the salt and herbs.
You can do this in a small bowl with a spoon, or grind them together in a mortar and pestle. As you combine them, imagine that there's a white light surrounding the mixture.

Take the mixture, and create a small ring on a plate or contained surface at your altar or sacred space. Inside the ring of salt, place your photo or drawing and close your eyes. Then put your hands over the setup, keeping your eyes closed, and imagine that there's a white light coming from the photo, surrounding you. Then say the following three times:

I am here,
I am surrounded
by light,
I am sacred,
and I protect
it all.

Repeat this spell whenever you feel
you need extra protection.

PROTECTION FROM BULLIES

THIS SPELL IS TO PROTECT YOUR ENERGY FROM BULLIES AND MAKE THEIR ENERGY AFFECT YOU LESS.

Day: Friday
Time: Night

Ingredients:
- Obsidian or another black stone
- Black cloth ▪ Rosemary ▪ Dill ▪ Twine

Start by laying out your black cloth on your altar or whatever sacred space you're going to be working at. Make sure the black cloth is flat, then gather the black stone and herbs in the middle of the fabric. While closing your eyes and envisioning a bubble around your body, fold up the cloth, with the herbs and stone in the center. The cloth should hold everything in while not being too bulky. Try to fold the cloth at least three times in each direction.

It's OK if you can't, but three is a protective number, and would further strengthen your intention if you are able to do this part. Once your cloth is neatly folded up, nice and secure, take your twine and wrap it around the cloth.

Make sure to wrap your twine moving away from your body, not toward it. Once your twine is securely holding the cloth package, tie three knots securing it together.

KEEP THIS CHARM IN YOUR POCKET WHILE AT SCHOOL, OR IN ANY OTHER SITUATION WHERE YOU FEEL AS THOUGH YOUR ENERGY IS BEING THREATENED BY BULLIES.

HOME/ROOM PROTECTION

THIS SPELL IS FOR PROTECTING HOMES OR ROOMS.

Day: Thursday
Time: Waning Moon or Dusk

You will need the following:
- Dash of salt • 3 pinches of rosemary
  • 3 pinches of garden sage • 3 pinches of pepper
  • 3 pinches of cayenne • A small blank sheet of white paper and a black pen • Olive oil • A jar (this can be an old jar you've washed or a new one—just make sure it's clean) • 1 white candle • White thread

The first step of this spell is to charge your ingredients. Hold each one while envisioning being protected. On the piece of paper with the black pen, write what you need specifically protected in your house, a personal symbol for protection, or just the word "protection." Fold the paper three times toward you. If you need it smaller, fold it again (three more times) toward you. Take the jar and fill it with herbs, crystals, and paper. Now fill the bottle with olive oil until it covers your ingredients.

Light the white candle and empower the contents of the bottle with the following words:

I charge you by
the Powers that be:
Protect my home
and family.
With my words
and all I do,
To this purpose
be Thee true.

Seal the bottle with its cork or lid. Tie the white ribbon around
the bottle. Knot it three times, as this is a powerful number.
When this is done, bury the bottle in your front yard near the front
door or place it somewhere safe in the heart of your home (a family
room, kitchen, dining room, or your bedroom) or on your altar.

PET PROTECTION SPELL

THIS SPELL IS FOR PROTECTING YOUR FURRY FRIENDS.

Day: Monday
Time: Morning or a Full Moon

You will need the following:
- Pet collar or name tag
- Cauldron or firesafe dish ▪ Salt
- Dill ▪ Lavender ▪ Peppercorn
- 1 white candle ▪ A sigil (a sign, word, or device) made by you

Cover the bottom of your dish or cauldron with a generous layer of salt. In the salt, draw the sigil you created using the line "**protection from harm for [pet's name].**" Next, layer your herbs and place your pet's item as a charm in the dish.

Place the white candle in the center of the collar or next to the name tag. Light the candle and repeat as follows:

Keep [pet's name]
safe from harm.
Let this spell be a barrier
with this charm.
To keep our family
safe and sound,
And always have them
homeward bound.

When the candle is *completely* out and no longer hot, place it near your pet. Repeat this spell as often as it feels right, or after any scary encounters with their safety.

PASSING A TEST

THIS SPELL IS FOR ACHIEVING WHAT YOU ARE
HOPING FOR!

Day: Monday
Time: Morning or Full Moon

For this spell, you will need:
- 1 orange candle or tealight
- Peppermint leaves
- An old pen for carving

Carve your candles with your intention. This can be done
either by carving sigils, or symbols, that correlate with
your intention or by directly writing what you are hoping
for! Surround your candle with peppermint leaves before
lighting it.

Take a moment to close your eyes and focus on why you
want to pass your test. No, it doesn't have to be something
beautiful and poetic; you can be quite direct with your
goals.

PAUSE ON THE IDEA; IMAGINE YOURSELF THERE,
HAVING ALREADY PASSED THE TEST. THERE IS
NO CHANT TO RECITE, JUST A FEW MOMENTS OF
PICTURING THIS SPELL ALREADY WORKING. ALLOW
THE CANDLES TO BURN OUT COMPLETELY.

MOON WATER

YOU CAN USE THIS WATER
TO FURTHER YOUR INTENTIONS.

Day: Any
Time: Full Moon

Ingredients:
- Drinking water
- 1 clear jar or bottle

The Moon is energetically
connected to the ocean tides and
the element of Water. Many believe
that Moon Water can harness the power
of the Moon to enhance intention setting. If you leave a
jar or a large bottle of water out overnight when there's a
Full Moon, you can then use the resulting Moon Water to
further your intentions. If, for example, you were trying to
be successful in something, you might drink a little Moon
Water in the morning while picturing yourself having the
success that you're looking for. Moon Water can be added
to anything, to further your intentions and to envision
success in just about anything.

LUCKY WISH

WISHING ON A DANDELION HAS A LOT MORE MAGICAL INTENTION BEHIND IT THAN YOU MIGHT THINK. THE PURPOSE OF THIS SPELL IS TO UTILIZE THAT MAGIC AND GAIN GOOD LUCK IN WHATEVER PROJECT YOU WANT TO SUCCEED IN. PERHAPS YOU WANT TO WIN A RAFFLE OR BE PICKED FOR A TEAM.

Day: Thursday
Time: Morning or Full Moon

You will need the following:
▪ Dandelion fluffs ▪ 1 bowl ▪ A second herb from your backyard or kitchen, aligned with your wish/intention

In a bowl, combine the dandelion fluffs and herbs. Refer to the apothecary chapter to find an herb suitable for your intention! Remember that magic is a unique practice that is strengthened by making it your own. Get creative. Holding your bowl, close your eyes and imagine your wish coming true. In your mind, it has already happened.

PUT THE MIXTURE INTO YOUR HAND, AND WHILE FACING THE DIRECTION OF THE SUN, CLOSE YOUR EYES AND BLOW THE MIXTURE AWAY FROM YOU.

BYE-BYE, BAD LUCK

SOMETIMES YOU FIND YOURSELF IN A SERIES OF
SITUATIONS THAT MAKE IT CLEAR YOU ARE HAVING
BAD LUCK. IT HAPPENS TO US ALL.

Day: Saturday
Time: New Moon or Night

Ingredients:
▪ Paper ▪ Black pen ▪ A green or blue candle

On a blank piece of paper, write down all the things
you can think of that have gone wrong for you
recently. Then take the paper and fold it away from
you two times. Place the paper under your
candle dish and light the candle, repeating
the following incantation four times:

Bad luck
of the recent past:
burn, burn away,
and turn to ash.

NIGHTMARES BE GONE!

NIGHTMARES CAN BE SCARY! THIS SPELL IS TO
HELP WARD OFF NIGHTMARES FROM RUINING
YOUR SLEEP.

Day: Any
Time: Before bed

You will need the following:
- A drinking glass half full of water

Place a glass half-filled with water near your bedside.
Swirl it five times counterclockwise, taking care not to
spill any, and say:

Nightmares,
bad dreams,
and feelings of dread:
enter this glass
and be held here
instead.

The next day, regardless of how you slept, pour
the water down the toilet and flush.
Rinse out the glass and leave it in the
bedroom, ready to be filled before
you go to sleep the following night.

LUCID DREAMING

LUCID DREAMING IS THE ACT OF BEING CONSCIOUS WHILE YOU DREAM. YOUR ABILITY TO MANIPULATE YOUR DREAMS WHILE ASLEEP IS SOMETHING THAT, FOR SOME PEOPLE, CAN BE TRULY FUN OR ENLIGHTENING.

Day: Any
Time: Before bed

All you need:
- Your intent • A piece of quartz (optional)

If you are using quartz, hold it in your hand and focus on pushing your intent into it. Out loud or in your head, repeat three times:

> Lucid dreams
> for me all right;
> I'll choose what I dream
> tonight.
> What I dream is up to me;
> I want this, so make it be.

You want to charge the crystal with this intent and then keep it on your nightstand or near where you sleep for the night. Alternatively, you can still use the chant by itself as a spell; your quartz is there as a physical placeholder, but it is optional.

FINDING YOUR VOICE

THIS SPELL WILL HELP YOU CHARM AN OBJECT TO WEAR OR KEEP IN YOUR POCKET, AND HELP YOU FIND COURAGE AND AMPLIFY YOUR VOICE.

Day: Friday
Time: Morning or Full Moon

You will need the following:
- A mixing jar ▪ A bottle you want to put it in
- ¼ cup of fractionated coconut oil or sweet almond oil
- 10 drops of sandalwood oil
- 3 clover buds ▪ 3 pinches of rosemary
- 3 pinches of crushed rose petals
- 3 pinches of marigold or calendula petals
- 7 red carnelian or jasper chips

Add all ingredients slowly, with the crystal chips being added last.

Hold the glass in your hands and envision a white light surrounding you and the jar. Envision the feeling of confidence and beauty or just a time when you felt at your most confident and strong.

Wear this charm whenever you need a confidence boost or have to do things that may otherwise make you feel shy.

MAKING NEW FRIENDS

MAKING NEW FRIENDS CAN BE SCARY AND HARD!
THIS SPELL WILL HELP GIVE YOU THE COURAGE
TO PUT YOURSELF OUT THERE AND MAKE NEW
FRIENDS!

Day: Friday
Time: Morning or Full Moon

You will need the following:
▪ A stone that feels nice in your hand, preferably
something smoothed by water ▪ Olive oil
▪ Flower petals ▪ Orange peels ▪ 1 bowl

In the bowl, combine the olive oil, orange peels, and
flower petals. Stirring the mixture clockwise, repeat
to yourself:

I attract people
who are like me.
I attract friendships
meant to last.
I attract connections
that are healthy.
I attract those who
will make me happy,
regardless
of our past.

Dipping your fingers into the oil and giving your hands a light oil coating, pick up the rock. Lightly coat the stone in the mixture: you are going to keep it in your pocket, so make sure not to put too much oil on it. Otherwise, it will make a mess. Close your eyes, and repeat the spell once more.

THIS STONE CAN THEN BE PLACED IN YOUR POCKET WHEN AT SCHOOL OR SOCIAL EVENTS, TO ATTRACT NEW FRIENDS.

MENDING A FRIENDSHIP

THIS SPELL IS TO HELP REPAIR A FRIENDSHIP THAT IS BROKEN. WHILE IT'S IMPORTANT TO REMEMBER THAT ALL MAGIC TAKES REAL-WORLD EFFORT AS WELL, THIS SPELL WILL HELP OPEN UP THE FRIENDSHIP TO THE ROAD TO HEALING.

Day: Friday
Time: Evening, Waxing, or Full Moon

Ingredients:
- A picture or drawing of each person, including yourself
- Two ribbons of different colors. I recommend picking two colors that represent both you and your friend.
- Honey ▪ A dish or plate

Start by placing the dish or plate on your altar for later. Take the two photos or drawings of you and your friend, then put them facing one another. Fold the photos toward you three times. Take the two ribbons and wrap them around the photos that you have just folded. Place your wrapped photos on the dish.

While putting a little honey on top of your photos, repeat the following words aloud three times:

BEING UNDERSTOOD BY OTHERS

USE THIS SPELL WHEN YOU FEEL INSECURE AND MISUNDERSTOOD BY OTHERS. IT WILL BRING YOU COURAGE AND CONFIDENCE IN YOUR ABILITIES.

Day: Thursday
Time: Morning, Waxing Moon, or Full Moon

You will need the following:
- Clover • Orange peel • Peppercorn
- Olive oil • Cinnamon • A bottle with a dropper

Wear this oil when you need a confidence boost. Combine all of the ingredients listed above into your bottle. Once combined, the bottle will sit on your altar for eleven days.

After it has sat there for eleven days, apply a drop to your wrist before going into any situation where you need a confidence boost, especially when you want to be heard.

USE THESE PAGES TO WRITE
LISTS OF THE INGREDIENTS YOU NEED
OR TO COMPOSE YOUR OWN SPELLS.